IPAD AIR 4 USE]

A complete step by step guide for Beginner and senior on how to use the new ipad air 4 with more than 30+ tips and tricks

BY

TOM O. HANK

Contents

INTRODUCTION

The iPad Air 2020 is a phenomenally well-made tablet that improves upon the next-gen version in a variety of ways and solves issues with the tablet's outdated design and accessories. The jump in price will make this more difficult for some, but the 2020 iPad Air is so impressive that you may have trouble deciding between it and the iPad Pro.

The iPad Air (2020) doesn't bring anything revolutionary to Apple's range of tablets, but keep in mind that many of the features previously only available on the iPad Pro are due to this much cheaper and therefore more attractive device.

While this is a tablet that probably doesn't alienate performance-hungry users from the iPad Pro, it does bring a lot with it that makes this range of tablets great for a cheaper device, if not as cheap as the standard range of iPad.

The iPad Air 4 is powered by Apple's new high-end A14 chipset, which is also the heart of the iPhone 12 series. It offers unmatched performance and ensures that the Air can comfortably perform any task you ask of it for demanding applications for streaming high-quality video.

There are two powerful speakers (although there are four speaker grilles) that will provide high-quality audio when watching videos or movies, and the rear camera has been upgraded to a 12-megapixel shooter.

Everything feels a little more refined on the iPad Air 4, so now it's hard to justify opting for an iPad Pro if you like this design but aren't desperate for a 120Hz display that updates quickly becomes.

If you need more storage or a slightly larger screen, consider the iPad Pro range. However, the 2020 iPad Air has been improved in almost every way imaginable, so it's hard to miss if you want a top-of-the-line iPad without spending a lot of money.

FEATURES OF IPAD AIR 4

Design

With a size of 10.9 inches (compared to 10.5 inches for the previous model iPad Air), the iPad Air 2020 has undergone a major redesign with an edge-to-edge display similar to the iPad Pro display. The aluminum case has flat, rounded edges that wrap around the retina display. This is a design that Apple first used on the iPad Pro.

Compared to an 11-inch iPad Pro, the iPad Air can hardly be distinguished apart from the slightly thicker body and the thicker frame around the screen.

iPad Pro left, iPad Air middle, iPad right

The iPad Air is 9.74 inches long and 7 inches wide, whereas the iPad Pro is 9.74 inches long and 7.02 inches extensive. The iPad Air is 6.1 mm dense and the 11-inch iPad Pro is 5.9 mm dense. The iPad Air weigh up 1 pound and the iPad Pro weighs up 1.04 pounds, so there isn't considerable of a change here.

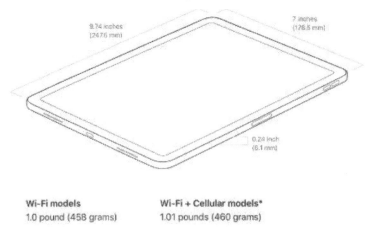

Wi-Fi models	Wi-Fi + Cellular models*
1.0 pound (458 grams)	1.01 pounds (460 grams)

Apple's previous iPad Air had smooth, tapered edges that were rounded, while the new design offers a flatter, more industrial look that goes with the iPad Pro and upcoming iPhone 12 models.

This is the first full-screen iPad Air and there is no Touch ID home button. However, there is no Face ID either, as biometric authentication is done via the new Touch ID fingerprint reader built into the top button. It scans a fingerprint-like the Touch ID home button, but it's smaller and more compact. The speakers and a microphone are on the top of the iPad Air, next to the Touch ID button.

On the right side of the iPad Air, there are volume buttons, a nano-SIM compartment for mobile models, and a magnetic space for charging the Apple Pencil. On the back, there is a rearview camera with a lens and a microphone. The single-lens camera is quite different from the square camera on the iPad

Pro in that it doesn't include a second camera or LiDAR scanner.

Stereo speakers and a USB-C port are located on the bottom of the iPad Air.

Colors

The aluminum case of the iPad Air is available in five colors. This is the first time Apple has offered an iPad in a lighter, non-traditional shade. IPad Air is accessible in silver, space gray, Rose gold, green, and sky blue.

The three lightest color options - rose gold, green, and sky blue - further differentiate the iPad Air 2020 from the iPad Pro 2020.

Touch ID

The iPad Air is the first iPad with Touch ID that is not integrated into the device's home button. Apple added Touch ID to the top button on the iPad Air, which enables Touch ID-based biometric authentication without the need for thick bezels to obscure the screen.

The top Touch ID button works the same as the Touch ID home button and can be used to unlock the iPad, access apps, shop with Apple

Pay, and more. The Touch ID on the iPad Air works in both portrait and landscape format.

Smart Connector

You can use the smart connector on the back of the iPad Air to communicate with and power accessories such as the magic keyboard. The Smart Connector interface can transfer power and data, so no batteries are vital for accessories that are connected to the iPad Air through the Smart Connector.

USB-C

The iPad Air is the second iPad after the iPad Pro that has been updated with a USB-C connector instead of a Lightning connector. The iPad Air can be connected to 4K or 5K USB-C displays, cameras, and other devices via the USB-C port. The USB-C port supports 5 Gbps data transfer and can charge an iPhone or Apple Watch with the right cable.

Display

The iPad Air comes with a 10.9-inch liquid retina display, which is identical to the iPad Pro display but does not offer 120 Hz ProMotion technology for a smoother scrolling experience.

It has a resolution of 2360 x 1640 at 246 pixels per inch and a total of 3.8 million pixels. Features full lamination (which reduces screen thickness and makes content appear more immersive), broad P3 color support for rich, true-to-life colors, anti-reflective coating with 1.8 percent reflectivity and 500 nit brightness, and True Tone support.

True Tone adjusts the white balance of the screen according to the ambient lighting to make the screen more pleasing to the eye. For example, if you are in a room with more yellow lighting, the iPad screen will be a warmer color, so there is not much contrast between the color of the iPad and the lighting in the area.

Apple Pencil support

Apple's newest iPad Air works with the second-generation Apple Pencil, which was originally released along with the iPad Pro in 2018. Until the introduction of the iPad Air, the second-generation Apple Pencil was limited to the iPad Pro models.

A14 chip

Apple uses its latest 5-nanometer chip technology in the iPad Air. The tablet is equipped with a 6-core A14 Bionic chip. Apple typically didn't use new chip technology in an iPad before debuting on an iPhone. However, it did so this year due to the delay in the launch of the iPhone 12 models. The iPhone 12 will also have the same A14 Bionic chip.

According to Apple, the A14 chip is equipped with 11.8 billion transistors, which increases its performance and energy efficiency. The 6-core plan of the A14 chip results in a 40 percent rise in GPU performance related to the A12 and the new 4-core GPU architecture results in a 30 percent development in graphics abilities related to the A12.

A leaked benchmark of the A14 chip confirms that the new fourth-generation iPad Air offers significant improvements over the previous generation model. It has a single-core score of 1583 and a multi-core score of 4198, which is much quicker than the single-core score of 1112 and the multi-core score of 2832 that the A12 Bionic chip has recorded in the iPad Air third age group.

1583	4198
Single-Core Score	Multi-Core Score

Neural engine

The A14 Bionic has a 16-core neural motor that is twice as fast and can perform up to 11 trillion operations per second to enable machine learning faster than ever before. The CPU similarly has second-generation machine knowledge accelerators for 10 times more rapidly machine learning calculations.

With the A14 chip with improved GPU and Neural Engine, Apple says the new iPad can deliver powerful new device experiences for image recognition, natural language learning, motion analysis, and more.

RAM

Based on the previously leaked A14 benchmark, it confirms that the iPad Air has 4GB of RAM, 1GB more than the 3GB of the previous generation model.

Camera

While there isn't a Face ID-compatible TrueDepth camera system on the iPad Air, there are 7-megapixel FaceTime HD f / 2.0 front cameras for selfies and video calls.

On the back of the iPad Air is a 12-megapixel wide-angle camera with a lens that is identical to the wide-angle camera used in the iPad Pro. Supports higher resolution videos and 4K video recordings compared to iPad Air anterior.

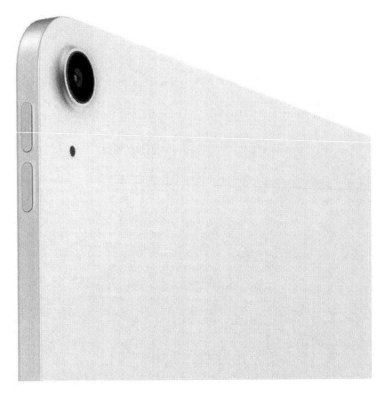

The 12-megapixel camera has an f/1.8 aperture for solid low-light performance, as well as all of the modern enhancements Apple has added to its device cameras, such as Live Photos with stabilization and autofocus with focus pixels, wide color recording, exposure control, Smart HDR, automatic image stabilization, noise reduction and more.

4K video recordings are supported at 20, 30, or 60 frames per second, as are slow-motion videos at 120 or 240 frames per second. The iPad Air can also record in 1080p at 30 or 60 frames per second and supports continuous autofocus, cinematic video stabilization, and the option to capture still images at 8 megapixels when recording 4K video.

Battery life

The iPad Air is equipped with a 28.6 watt-hour lithium polymer battery, which, according to Apple, lasts up to 10 hours when surfing the Internet via WLAN or when watching videos.

Cellular models last up to nine hours when you browse the Internet using a cellular connection. IPad Air can be charged with the included 20W USB-C power adapter and USB-C to USB-C cable.

Other features

Microphones and speakers

The iPad Air has binary sets of speakers for stereo sound in portrait and landscape setup. Two microphones are included for calls, video and audio recordings.

Sensors

In addition to a Touch ID sensor, the iPad Air has a three-axis gyroscope, accelerometer, barometer, and ambient light sensor for True Tone and other functions.

Support WiFi 6 and Bluetooth

The iPad Air 2020 supports WiFi 6, also known as 802.11ax. The updated standard offers faster speeds, improved network capacity, better energy efficiency, lower latency, and improved connectivity when multiple WiFi devices are in the same area.

WiFi 6 devices also support WPA3, a security protocol that offers improved cryptographic strength. It also supports Bluetooth 5.0.

Gigabit LTE

Gigabit-class LTE is available for iPad Air cellular models, and the LTE modem chip is similar to the chip found in the iPad Pro.

There are two SIM options on iPad Air: a physical nano-SIM slot on the side of the device and an eSIM or digital SIM card that is designed to work without a physical SIM card.

The physical nano-SIM slot is compatible with Apple SIM, which allows users to switch providers seamlessly. Many carriers in the US and other countries support Apple SIM, but those who don't, like Verizon, still require a physical SIM card.

Storage space

Apple sells the iPad Air with 64GB of storage or 256GB of storage with no 128GB mid-tier storage selection accessible.

Accessories

Magic Keyboard and Trackpad support

Like the iPad Pro, the iPad Air also works with the Magic Keyboard, which was introduced in early 2020. The Magic Keyboard is a folio case with a fully illuminated keyboard and, for the first time, a trackpad.

The Magic keyboard uses scissor-type mechanisms, similar to the keyboard on the MacBook Air and MacBook Pro. The scissor mechanism offers 1mm of travel, which Apple says is the best typing experience on the iPad.

The Magic Keyboard is magnetically connected to the iPad Air and has cantilevered hinges that work on a desk or lap. The hinges allow viewing angle adjustments of up to 130 degrees so that they can be adjusted for any usage situation. The design of the Magic Keyboard allows the iPad to "float" in the air, with the bottom of the case sloping back in keyboard mode.

When not in use, the keyboard's folio design holds the iPad Air securely and covers the front and back of the device. The Magic keyboard has a USB-C port for inductive USB-C charging functions so that the integrated USB-C port on the iPad Air remains free for accessories such as external drives and displays.

Apple pencil

IPad Air 2020 models are compatible with the second-generation Apple Pencil. The Apple Pencil is $ 129 and attaches to the iPad Air with magnets. When attached magnetically, it is inductively charged. Pairing is also done via the magnet attachment.

The second-generation Apple Pencil offers gesture support. With a tap of your finger, you can switch brushes or quickly switch from a brush to an eraser without picking up the pen and choosing a new tool.

The Apple Pencil works on the iPad Air with its own and third-party applications. It offers advanced palm repellency, extreme precision, and imperceptible lag for a paper-like writing experience that third-party pens cannot match.

The pressure mount allows you to draw thinner and thicker lines by increasing the pressure on the iPad screen. Side spring detection enables shading when the Apple Pencil is tilted.

SET UP THE IPAD

Turn on your new iPad and organize it via an internet connection. You can also configure the iPad by connecting it to your computer. If you have another iPad or Android device, you can relocate your data to your new iPad.

Prepare to install

To make the setup as easy as possible, the following elements are available:

- An Internet connection through a Wi-Fi network (you may need the network name and password) or a mobile data service through an operator (Wi-Fi + Cellular models)
- Your Apple ID and PIN; If you don't have an Apple ID, you can generate one during setup

- Your credit or debit card account data if you want to add a card to Apple Pay during setup
- Your old iPad or a backup of your device when you transfer your data to your new device
- Your Android device when you transfer your Android content

Turn on your iPad and configure it

1. Press and hold the upper button till you see the Apple symbol.

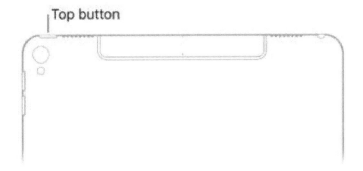

If the iPad won't turn on, you may need to charge the battery.

2. Do one of the following:

- Touch Configure manually and follow the on-screen instructions to set it up.
- If you have another iPhone, iPad, or iPod touch with iOS 11, iPadOS 13, or later, you can use Quick Launch to set up your new device automatically. Bring the two devices closer together and follow the on-screen instructions to securely copy many of your settings, preferences, and iCloud keychain. You can then reestablish the rest of your data and content to your new device from your iCloud backup.

If both devices have iOS 12.4, iPadOS 13, or later, you can wirelessly transfer all of your data from your old device to your new one.

31

Keep your devices close together and connected until the migration process is complete.

You can also transfer your data between your devices using a cable connection.

- If you're blind or visually impaired, triple-click the Start button (on an iPad with a Home button) or triple-click the top button (on other iPad models) to turn on VoiceOver, the screen reader. You can also double-tap the screen with three fingers to activate the zoom.

Change from an Android device to an iPad

The first time you set up your new iPad, you can automatically and safely transfer your data from an Android device.

Note: You can only use the Move to iOS app the first time you set up an iPad. When you're done with the setup and want to use Move to iOS, you'll need to erase your iPad and start over or move your data manually.

1. On your device with Android version 4.0 or later, download the Move to iOS app.

2. On your iPad, do the following:

- Follow the setup wizard.
- On the Apps & data display, touch Move data from Android.

3. On the Android device, do the following:

- Turn on Wi-Fi.
- Open the Move to iOS app.
- Follow the instructions on the screen.

33

WHAT IS NEW IN IPADOS 14

Widgets

Redesigned widgets

Widgets have been reformed to be better-looking and more data-rich, making them even more beneficial throughout the day.

Widgets of different sizes

Widgets are now available in small, regular, and large sizes so you can first-rate the number of facts that are right for you.

Widget Gallery

The central place for all Apple and third-party widgets. The gallery shows the main widgets based on what users install and use most often.

Smart stack

In the Widget Gallery, you can select Smart Stack, a group of widgets that uses device intelligence to display the right widget at the right time based on factors such as time, location, and activity. For example, you can view news in the morning, calendar events during the day, and a summary of activities during the night.

Siri Suggestions Widget

The Siri Suggestions widget uses information on your device to specify actions you can take based on your usage forms, such as ordering a coffee or starting a podcast. Touch the suggestion to take the action without starting the application.

Developer API

Developers can generate their widgets using a new API that permits them to take benefit of newly designed widgets, including the capacity to display them on the home screen and display them at the right time.

Application design

Reformed sidebars

The sidebars have been redesigned with a new look that offers even more information and at the same time shows more application functions in the main window. Photos, music, shortcuts, voice memos, calendars, notes, files, emails, and contacts have redesigned the sidebars to provide a unified iPadOS experience.

Toolbars

Optimized toolbars in calendars and files allow applications to group buttons and menus into a single bar at the top of the application so that all controls are easily accessible.

Popovers

Pop-ups are automatically discarded when you interact with other parts of an application.

Dropdown menus

There are new drop-down menus in built-in applications, e.g. Files, allowing you to access application functions with a single button.

Date picker

A redesigned date picker makes it easier to select dates in the calendar and contacts. It will show up as a calendar so you can just touch the date you want.

Search

Top hit results

The most relevant results, including map apps, contacts, skills, POIs, and websites, are shown at the top, making it easy to find what you need.

Fast launcher

Enter a few characters and you can quickly launch apps and websites by tapping go.

Compact UI

New compact designs take up only the required space and allow you to search from anywhere, e.g. For example, from the home screen or in any application so that you don't lose sight of what you are doing.

Look for suggestions as you type

Just start typing and search suggestions will appear below the search box.

Search in the app

Start a search in applications such as Mail, Messages, and Files.

Web search

Searching the web is now easier than ever. Start inputting and see pertinent websites and web search suggestions above. This is a quick and easy way to launch Safari for a comprehensive web search.

Compact user interface

Calls

When you get a call from your iPad, it will seem like a banner instead of captivating up the whole screen so you don't lose track of what you are doing. Swipe up on the banner to close it or down to access advanced phone features.

Third-party VoIP calls

There is a developer API that applications like Skype can use to support compact incoming calls.

FaceTime calls

When you obtain a FaceTime call, it seems like a banner instead of captivating up the entire screen. Swipe up on the banner to close it or swipe down to access advanced FaceTime features.

Siri

Siri has a wholly new solid design that permits you to see the information on the screen and easily start your next task. When you start a request, Siri will appear in the lower right corner of the screen. The results have been updated to give you the information you need in a new compact design. And Siri rapidly gets out of the way when launching apps, making calls, or getting tips.

Scribble

Write by hand in any text field

With Scribble, you can hand-write directly in a text box with Apple Pencil, and the font is converted to typescript. The transcription is done on your device so all your writing remains private.

Scratches to erase

New editing gestures make writing and editing easier. Just scratch a word or space to erase it.

Circle to choose from

Circle a word to select it. This is ideal when you need to copy or move a word.

Hold to add space

Tap and hold among words to add space with your Apple Pencil.

Scribble the shortcut palette

The shortcuts palette is where you find the most frequently used actions for the application you are using, so you can tap the palette without using the on-screen keyboard. For example, when you type mail, the Shortcuts palette gives you options for choosing fonts and inserting pictures so you can quickly tap the option you want. Under Reminders, you will find options for recent location and time settings that you may need when creating reminders.

Chinese support for Scribble

Write in Simplified or Traditional Chinese with Scribble. Scribble also supports a combination of Chinese and English so you can write English and Chinese words together without having to switch languages. It's a seamless experience that is as easy as handwriting.

Better take notes with Apple Pencil

Smart selection

Use Smart Picker to pick out a single handwritten word or to complete sentences with the same gestures you've always used for written text. Double-tap a word and three-tap a phrase to select a phrase.

Smart selection: Drag to select

Slide your Apple Pencil or your finger over your handwriting to select entire paragraphs in one movement. Speed up the selection of large sections of handwriting and slow down for greater precision. The slower you move, the more accurate the selection, so you can even picks individual letters. If you have picked too much, just sweep back to deselect

46

the words. Machine learning ensures that your handwriting is chosen instead of your drawings and doodles.

Copy and paste as text

Select your handwritten notes to choose Copy as Text, and when you paste them, they become typed text. The rehabilitated text recalls the setup of the unique handwritten notes, making it perfect for anyone who prefers handwritten notes but wants a digitized copy. The transcription is done on your device so all your writing remains private.

Make space

Add or eradicate spaces between sentences or paragraphs in your handwritten notes by first choosing the text, then dragging the slight triangle on the left up or down with your Apple Pencil or your finger. You can also use the new Insert Space Above option in the Call Bar, which displays a horizontal line that you can drag to add as much or as little space as you need.

Data detectors

Do more with your handwritten notes. The device's intelligence recognizes addresses, phone numbers, email addresses, and other data so you can take action on your handwritten notes. Just tap the detected data and you can choose from actions that you can take, such as opening a building window in Mail or viewing an address in Maps.

Design recognition

Shape Recognition lets you draw geometrically faultless lines, curves, and shapes, together with hearts, stars, and arrows. Just start drawing and take a short break at the end. Its imperfect shape becomes perfect. Shape recognition is great for drawing quick diagrams and sketches.

Augmented reality

ARKit: Depth API

The Depth API provides accurate depth measurements that are captured by the LiDAR scanner so that virtual objects can interact with the real world exactly as expected. This detailed information also opens up new use cases in AR applications, e.g. precise body

49

measurements for precise virtual tests or advanced photo and video editing effects.

ARKit: location anchor

Augmented Reality experiences can be placed at specific geographic coordinates so that you can see them in some of your favorite places around the world - in every city, next to famous places, and even in your neighborhood.

ARKit: Extended support for face tracking

Even more, users can enjoy AR experiences that are only accessible through the front camera, with expanded support for face tracking on the 12.9-inch iPad Pro (3rd generation) and later, and on the iPad Pro 11-inch and later.

RealityKit: Video textures

Video qualities can be added to several portions of an actual scene or article in RealityKit to bring actual objects, surfaces, and characters to life.

RealityKit: Improved object occlusion

With the LiDAR scanner information built into RealityKit and enhanced edge detection, virtual objects in the AR Quick Look and RealityKit experiences interact exactly as you'd expect and can be realistically obscured by physical objects for the first time.

Messages

Pinned conversations

Put your favorite chats at the top of your chat list so you can always access them. The latest news, tap backs and tip indicators are animated via the pin. If you set up a group conversation, three current participants will circle the marker when you send a message.

Up to nine pins

You can have up to nine pinned chats that sync among messages on iOS, iPadOS, and macOS.

Mentions

Address a message to someone in a group conversation by typing the person's name. You can customize a particularly active group so that notifications are only received when mentioned.

Inline answers

You can now answer straight to an exact message in a group chat. View all related posts in their view to keep track of a thread.

Set group photo

Set up an image for your group conversation with a photo, emoji, or emoji that is shared with everyone in the group.

Memoji

New hairstyles

Modify your Memoji with 11 new hairstyles together with a men's bun, topknot, and a modest side part.

New types of hats

Show off your hobby or job with 19 new hat styles, including a bike helmet, nurse hat, and swim cap.

New Memoji stickers

With three new Memoji stickers you can send your friends a hug, a slap, or even a blush.

More expressive emoji

The renewed face and muscle structure makes the Memoji and Memoji stickers even more expressive.

More age options

With six new stage selections, you can modify your look whether you're having a baby, in your golden years, or anywhere in between.

Hairstyles with fades

Thirteen hairstyles now have fades in which the hair gradually tapers on the side of the face so that it reflects your style.

Face coverings

Customize your Memoji to suit your appearance with new face covering, including color.

Maps

Manual

Get commendations on the finest places to go
to a city with guides formed by a collection of
trusted brands. Guides help you discover great
places to eat, shop, meet friends, or explore
cities around the world. You can save the
instructions for future reference. They're
automatically updated as new places are
added so you always have the latest
recommendations.

Cycle

Maps now guide cyclists on bike lanes, bike
lanes, and bike-friendly roads. Preview the
elevation of your ride, see how difficult a road
is, and set routes to avoid steep slopes or

stairs. Maps also offer personalized voice directions and a full Apple Watch experience that lets you navigate at a glance.

Routing of electric vehicles

Certainly idea trips with your electric vehicle. Maps automatically add charging stops along your route and even take the charging time into account when calculating the ETA. Once you've securely added your electronic vehicle to your iPad, Maps can, for instance, keep track of the present charge and type of charge to find the best way for your vehicle.

Congestion zones

Big cities like London and Paris have congestion zones to reduce traffic in dense areas. Maps allow you to view the tolls in the congestion zone on the map and move around them if you want.

New map available in more countries

Our new map will hit more countries later this year, including Canada, Ireland, and the UK. The new map provides more detailed information on streets, buildings, parks, marinas, beaches, airports, and more, and gives you a more realistic view of the world.

Access to registration

In cities in China that restrict driving through dense urban areas, your vehicle authorization can determine whether you have access. Put your license plate number on the maps to see if you can travel through the area. License plate information is securely stored on maps and never leaves your device.

Home

Proposed automation

When you add a new accessory, the Home app suggests helpful ways to do it automatically. For example, you can let your porch lights go on every night, open your garage door when you get home, and more.

Home status

A new visual rank at the top of the Home app gives you a summary of accessories that require your attention, have significant status changes to share, or can be rapidly monitored.

Home controller

The home controls in the Control Center now energetically suggest the most pertinent accessories and scenes that you are likely to want to control, based on the time of day and the occurrence with which you classically use them. For example, you might see controls for bedroom lights and a good morning scene, or controls for door lock and exterior lights when you come home at night. You can also touch the Home icon to view other accessories and scenes.

Adaptive lighting for smart light bulbs

Color changing lights can be adjusted automatically throughout the day to maximize comfort and productivity. You can start the morning with warmer colors, stay focused and alert at noon with cooler colors, and relax at night by eliminating blue light.

Face recognition for cameras and doorbells

In addition to recognizing people, animals, and vehicles, security cameras can identify the people you've tagged in the Photos app for fuller activity notifications. Easily tag people and choose if you want to receive notifications based on the person.

Activity zones for cameras and doorbells

With HomeKit Secure Video, you can define activity areas in the view of a camera to record videos or receive notifications when motion is detected in these areas.

Safari

Favorites in standard registers

Page icons are displayed in tabs by default, so you can see open tabs at a glance.

Website translation

Easily translate entire web pages in Safari. If a compatible webpage is found, Safari will display a translation icon in the address field. Just touch to interpret into English, Spanish, Simplified Chinese, French, German, Russian, or Brazilian Portuguese.

Website privacy report

Tap the Privacy Report button to access a privacy report that shows all of the cross-location trackers that Smart Tracking Prevention has blocked in Safari.

Password monitoring

Safari securely monitors your saved passwords and automatically searches for any passwords that may have been involved in a data breach. To this end, Safari uses strong cryptographic techniques to regularly check your password derivations against a list of broken passwords securely and privately that even Apple does not reveal your password information. If Safari detects a violation, it can help you update to Sign in to Apple, if available, or automatically generate a new strong password.

Performance

With an ultra-fast JavaScript machine, Safari is the wildest tablet browser in the world and beats Windows browsers in a benchmark for the benchmark.

AirPods

Spatial audio

Spatial Audio with dynamic head tracking brings the cinematic experience straight to your AirPods Pro. By relating directional audio filters and delicately modifying the occurrences each ear takes, Spatial Audio can place sounds almost anywhere in the room. Create an Immersive Surround Sound Experience. Using the gyroscope and accelerometer on your AirPods Pro and iPad, spatial audio tracks the movement of your head and device, compares movement data, and reassigns the sound field so it stays anchored to your device even after your head moves.

Headphone accommodation

This new accessibility feature is designed to magnify soft sounds and regulate specific frequencies for a person's hearing to help keep music, movies, phone calls, and podcasts sounding clearer, more clear and familiarize the noises in your environment to your hearing needs.

Automatic device switching

AirPods automatically switch between your iPhone, iPad, iPod touch, and Mac paired with the same iCloud account, making using your AirPods with your Apple devices even easier.

65

Battery messages

Battery alerts let you know when you need to charge your AirPods.

AirPods Pro Motion API

The Motion API gives creators access to AirPods Pro guides, user acceleration, and revolution rates, perfect for fitness apps, games, and more.

Siri

Compact user interface

Siri has an all-new compact design that lets you review the information on the screen and get started on your next task smoothly. When you start a request, Siri will appear in the lower right corner of the screen. The results have been updated to give you the information you need in a new compact design. And Siri rapidly gets out of the way when beginning apps, making calls or getting information.

Extended knowledge

Siri has significantly expanded its knowledge with 20 times more data than it did three years ago.

Web responses

Siri can now assist you to find solutions to a wider range of questions using facts from the Internet, so you can get solutions without surfing the Internet

Additional translation languages

Siri can translate between many more languages and supports more than 65 language pairs.

Cycling direction

Now you can ask Siri for directions.

Share ETA

While navigating Apple Maps, you can ask Siri to share your ETA with a contact.

The new voice in more languages

Siri's new voice uses advanced neural text-to-speech technology to create an incredibly natural sound. The new voice was previously available in US English and is available in several additional regions.

Send audio messages

You are now ready to send audio messages using Siri. This is ideal if you want to make your messages more expressive. Third-party messaging apps are compatible with SiriKit.

Privacy

Data protection information in the App Store

A new section on each product page in the App Store allows you to view a summary of the app's privacy practices before downloading it. Developers report their privacy practices themselves, including those used by the developer and used to track it across all organizations, in a simple and easy-to-read format.

App tracking controls and transparency

The developer must get your permission before they can pursue them. Take a look at the apps that you have permitted to track so you can change your settings.

Approximate location

A new setting allows you to choose whether to share your approximate location with an application instead of your exact location.

Limited access to the photo library

You can choose to share only particular items with a developer who requests access to your photos, or you can permit access to your full library.

Recording indicator

iPadOS shows an indicator when an app is using the microphone or camera, both in the app and in Control Center.

Update to sign in to Apple

Developers can compromise the option to advance current app accounts to sign in to Apple so users can enjoy more privacy, safety, and ease of use without having to set up a new account.

Accessibility

VoiceOver detection

On-Device Intelligence senses key elements that seem on the screen to add VoiceOver support for applications and web experiences that don't have built-in ease of access support.

VoiceOver detection - picture descriptions

A voiceOver reads full-sentence descriptions from pictures and photos in apps and on the web.

VoiceOver Recognition: Text recognition

VoiceOver speaks the text it identifies in pictures and photos.

VoiceOver Detection: Screen Detection

VoiceOver automatically detects interface controls to help you navigate and access your applications.

Headphone accommodation

This new accessibility feature is designed to magnify soft sounds and regulate specific frequencies for a person's hearing to help keep music, movies, phone calls, and podcasts sounding clearer, more audible and adapt the noises in your environment to your hearing needs.

Sound detection

Sound detection uses information on the device to notify users who may otherwise miss audible environmental alerts in their area. On the iPhone, iPad, or iPod touch, users are notified when a certain type of sound or alarm is detected, such as a phone call a fire alarm, or a buzzer.

Familiarity with sign language

FaceTime can notice when a member is using sign language and focus the person in a FaceTime group call.

App clips

A new way to discover applications

An application clip is a small part of an application that can be recognized when needed and focuses on a specific task.

Quickly available

The app clips are inherently small so they can be used in just a few seconds. They are not installed like apps. When you stop using them, they just go away.

Discover at the right time

Search for app clips by scanning QR codes from Messages, Maps, and Safari, and via Apple-designed app clip codes that are uniquely linked to each app clip.

Discover: Scan a QR code

QR codes can start a related app clip when you scan them with the QR code reader or the camera app.

Explore: Tap a link in Safari

Links posted on the web can launch a related application clip from Safari.

Discover: Start in Maps

For locations that support app clips, the place card in Maps has a launch button.

Discover: Open in messages

App clips are easy to share and can be opened in messages. When you get one, you can start it right there.

Discover: App Clip Codes

App clip codes are Apple-designed identifiers that are uniquely combined with specific app clips and provide an easy way to find and launch an app experience exactly where and when you need it. You can scan an application clip code with your camera. We'll be supporting them in an iPadOS 14 software update later this year.

Download the full application

After using an app clip, you can download the full version of the app with just one tap.

Works with Apple Pay

App clips can use Apple Pay to make purchases without entering credit card information.

Works with Sign in with Apple

App clips can use Sign In with Apple to deliver personalized experiences without entering separate account information.

App store

Application details

See key details about each application in a scrollable, displayable view that shows customer reviews, application age rating, category, game controller support for games, and more.

Friends play recommendations

Find out what games your Game Center friends are playing. You can now see your friends on any Game Center-enabled gaming product page and tap to view their Game Center profile.

Family subscriptions

Now you can share App Store subscriptions with all family members in one purchase. Participating app subscriptions can be shared with members of your Family Sharing group.

Apple Arcade

Achievements

Visit the Apple Arcade game pages to explore the objectives and milestones you can unlock in the games and see your progress.

Keep playing

Start the games you recently played on your devices from the Apple Arcade tab.

Show and filter all games

Search the entire Apple Arcade catalog. Sort and filter by release date, updates, category, driver support, and more.

Game Center Game Control Panel

The game board shows you and your friend's progress at a glance. Quickly access your Game Center profile, achievements, leaderboards, and more, right from the game.

Upcoming

Check out the upcoming Apple Arcade games and download them as soon as they are released.

Apple Cash family

Activate Apple Cash for family members under the age of 18

Just add them to your Apple Cash account using Family Sharing. You can activate Apple Cash for up to five family members.

Send your kids money for chores, housework, or just for fun

Send money instantly, in messages, or by asking Siri. There is no app to download as Apple Cash is located on your iPad under

Settings> Wallet & Apple Pay. And the configuration is very simple.

Set restrictions and view activities

With maternal controls, you can limit who your kids can send money to. Get complete transparency and receive notifications of in-person purchases or payments with Apple Pay as soon as they occur.

Limit access and keep the funds safe

As easy as granting access, you can also restrict use. Turn off Apple Cash for a family member that you've turned it on for. Once deactivated, your Apple Cash balance will be securely locked until you grant access again.

Stock supervision

Let another adult in your Family Sharing group see the activities of all family members for whom you have Apple Cash enabled.

Camera

Quick changes in video mode

All iPad models now have quick switches to change the video resolution and frame rate in video mode.

Mirror photos were taken with the front camera

A new option in Settings lets you take mirrored selfies that mirror the front camera preview.

Improvements in reading QR codes

Improvements in reading QR codes make it easier to read codes, even if they are small or concerned objects.

FaceTime

Improved video quality

FaceTime offers improved video quality with up to 1080p resolution on a 10.5-inch iPad Pro, 11-inch iPad Pro (1st generation) and higher, and 12.9-inch iPad Pro (2nd generation) and later.

Familiarity with sign language

FaceTime can notice when a member is using sign language and focus the person in a FaceTime group call.

Family

Share subscriptions to third-party applications

Developers can support Family Sharing for in-app purchases and subscriptions so that all members of your family can access it with a single purchase from the App Store.

Files

Reformed sidebar

Files contain a completely redesigned sidebar in which all core functions are combined in one central location. Access current files, shared documents, external drives, file servers, and favorite folders with just one touch of a button.

Support for APFS encrypted drives

The Files application supports external drives that use APFS encryption. Simply enter the password to access the contents of the drive.

International

New bilingual dictionaries

The new bilingual dictionaries include French - German, Indonesian - English, Japanese - Simplified Chinese, and Polish - English.

Auto-correction support for Ireland and Norway

AutoCorrect now supports Irish Gaelic and Norwegian Nynorsk.

Kana keyboard redesigned for Japan

Write numbers with repetitive digits more easily in the redesigned Numbers and Symbols layer on the Japanese Kana keyboard.

Full-screen effects localized for India

Messages now have conforming full-screen effects when directing greetings in 22 Indian languages.

Wubi keyboard for China

You can use the Wubi input method on your iPad so that users who are familiar with the input method can type faster than ever before.

New sources for India

The new fonts for India include 20 new fonts for documents. Also, 18 existing fonts have been updated with more weights and italics to give you more options.

Email support for non-Latin language email addresses

You can send and receive an email with addresses in non-Latin languages, including Chinese, Japanese, Korean, Russian, Thai, and Hindi.

88

Keyboard

Dictation on the device

Keyboard dictation improves with the use of your device and becomes more personalized over time. The dictation on the device protects your privacy by taking all processing completely offline. The search dictation uses a server-based dictation.

Emoji popup menu

The new emoji popover lets you type emoji when using a hardware keyboard with your iPad.

Autocomplete contacts in third party apps

Instead of sharing your whole contact list in third-party applications, you can now enter specific names to mechanically fill in the suitable phone numbers, addresses, or email addresses in the fields where they are requested. Auto-complete are done on your device and contacts are not shared with third-party inventors without your agreement.

Auto-correction support for Ireland and Norway

AutoCorrect now supports Irish Gaelic and Norwegian Nynorsk.

Kana keyboard redesigned for Japan

Write numbers with repetitive digits more easily in the redesigned Numbers and

Symbols layer on the Japanese Kana keyboard.

Wubi keyboard for China

You can use the Wubi input method on your iPad so that users who are familiar with the input method can type faster than ever before.

Music

Listen now

The new home page in Apple Music is designed to play and discover your favorite music, artists, playlists, and mixes in one place. Listen now begins with an overview of your top options based on your musical interests. As you play, Apple Music learns what you like and organizes suggestions.

Autoplay

Now Apple Music continues to play. When you reach the end of a song or playlist, Autoplay will search for similar songs so the music will keep playing.

Improved search

An entirely new search shows music by genre, mood, and activity. Helpful tips appear as you type to find exactly what you're looking for.

Library filtering

Find artists, albums, playlists, and other kinds of stuff in your library even quicker. Swipe down on each section to filter your results.

Text and Queue in full-screen mode

Follow your favorite music with perfectly synchronized full-screen texts and manage playback more easily, all beautifully redesigned for the iPad.

Photos

Filter and sort

You can filter your group by Favorites, Edited, Videos, and Photos. And you can sort any of your albums, including shared albums, oldest or newest first.

Easy and fluid navigation

Just zoom in and out for quick access to the photos and videos you're looking for in more views of photos, including albums, favorites, media types, shared albums, and more.

Stabilization of the playback of live photos

Live photos were taken with iPadOS 14 autoplay with boosted equilibrium in the Years, Months, and Days views.

Add context to pictures and videos with subtitles

View and edit subtitles to add background to your pictures and videos. Easily find the captions you added on the Find tab. When iCloud Photos is turned on, caption sync seamlessly across all of your devices.

Memory expansion

Enjoy a more relevant selection of photos and videos in Memories, improved video stabilization when playing a memory movie, a larger selection of music tracks that automatically adjust to the length of your memory movie, and improved framing when switching between movies Horizontal and vertical orientation.

Redesigned image selection in apps

With the redesigned Image Picker, it's easier than ever to find and select the images you want in apps like Messages, Email, and Safari, as well as third-party apps. Use the similar Smart Search in the Photos app to find just the pictures and videos you are looking for and first-rate numerous pictures with ease.

Podcasts

Smarter listen now

Listen now includes a new Up Next - your episode queue so you can easily pick up where you left off. Find the latest episodes of shows you already love or discover a new episode chosen just for you.

Reminders

Assign reminders

Assign reminders to the people you share lists with and they will receive a reminder.

New reminders from the list screen

Create a new reminder on iPad right from the list screen without entering a specific list.

Smart suggestions for dates and places

Reminders automatically suggest the date, time, and place for a reminder based on similar reminders you've created in the past.

Edit multiple reminders at the same time

Easily fill, mark, or change the date and time for multiple reminders at once.

Custom lists with emoji

Customize the look of your lists with newly added emojis and symbols.

Email reminder tips

When you communicate with someone in Mail, Siri detects possible reminders and suggests you believe them.

Organize smart lists

Personalize the reminder app the way you want by rearranging or hiding smart lists.

Improved search

Find the right reminders by searching for people, places, and even detailed notes you've added.

Improved calendar selection

With the new calendar menu, choose the right date and time for reminders. You can quickly view the entire month and easily scroll through months and years.

The settings

Set default email and browser apps

Set a default web browser and email application to launch when you touch a link or compose a new email message.

Shortcuts

Redesigned iPad app

The Shortcuts app has been restyled for the iPad and comprises a new sidebar, simplified shortcut editor, and support for numerous windows.

Automation tips

Shortcuts now suggest mechanizations based on your usage designs, making it relaxed than ever to get started.

Folder

You can easily organize your shortcuts with folders. Each folder can be added as a widget on the home screen.

Compact design

When you launch a shortcut from the shortcuts app, Siri Suggestions, Share Sheet, Accessibility Features, or the new shortcut

100

widget on the home screen, it now has a new, compact design so you stay in context.

New automation triggers

Make shortcuts based on getting an electronic mail or message, sleep mode, the device's battery level, closing an application, or connecting or disconnecting the device. And the time of day activates can now run without user approval.

Voice memos

Folder

You can use folders to record your voice memos.

Smart folders

Smart folders mechanically group Apple Watch recordings, freshly erased recordings, and favorites.

Favorites

Mark recordings as favorites for quick access later.

Enhance the recording

Improve Recording lessens contextual noise and room echo with one touch.

CONNECT THE IPAD TO THE INTERNET

Connect your iPad to the internet using an available Wi-Fi network. Wi-Fi + cellular replicas can similarly connect to the Internet using a cellular network.

Connect the iPad to a Wi-Fi network

1. Go to Settings> WiFi and enable WiFi.

2. Touch one of the following options:

- **A network:** Enter the PIN if essential.
- **Others:** Join a hidden network. Enter the hidden network name, security type, and password.

If you can see the Wi-Fi icon at the top of the screen, the iPad is connected to a Wi-Fi network. (To confirm, open Safari to view a webpage.) IPad will recouple when you return to the same position.

Join a personal hotspot

If an iPad (Wi-Fi + cellular) shares a personal hotspot, you can use your cellular internet connection.

Go to Settings> Wi-Fi and select the name of the device that is sharing the personal hotspot.

If your iPad prompts you for a password, enter the password shown in Settings> Cellular> Personal Hotspot on the device sharing the personal hotspot.

Connect the iPad to a cellular network (Wi-Fi + cellular replicas)

Your iPad automatically connects to the mobile data network of your network operator if no Wi-Fi network is available. If the iPad can't connect, check the following:

1. Check that your SIM card is activated and unlocked.

2. Go to Settings> Cellular Data.

3. Make guaranteed cellular data is twisted on.

If you need an internet connection, the iPad will do the following until it is connected:

- Try to connect to the most recently used available Wi-Fi network
- Displays a list of Wi-Fi networks in range and connects to one of your choices
- Establishes a connection to the mobile data network of your operator (Wi-Fi + cellular models)

105

Note: If a Wi-Fi connection to the Internet is not available, applications and services can transmit data over your operator's cellular network, which can incur additional charges. Contact your provider for information about your mobile data tariffs.

HOW TO ALLOCATE EVERYTHING FROM AN OLD IPAD TO A NEW IPAD

You've just upgraded to a new iPad and want to move all of your apps, pictures, settings, and data from an old iPad to the new iPad, right? If you're just doing this, you can go the Post-PC route with iCloud (recommended) or the old route with iTunes, we'll show you both.

Use iCloud to transfer data from the old iPad to the new one

Using iCloud is by far the easiest method, but of course iCloud must be set up and configured for this to work. This is the post-pc method.

From the old iPad

1. Launch Settings and tap iCloud. Then tap on "Storage & Backup".
2. Tap Back Up Now to start a manual iCloud backup
3. Let the backup finish and leave the old iPad alone

Your work on the old iPad is done. Now take the new iPad and turn it on.

From the new iPad

1. On the Configure iPad screen, choose to Restore from iCloud Backup and tap next.

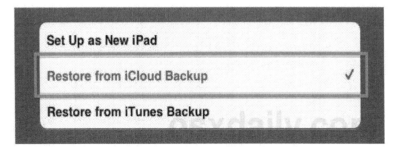

2. Sign in to your iCloud account and choose the most recent backup of the old iPad that you just made

3. Tap "Restore" to transfer the backup data from the old iPad to the new iPad

The duration of the transfer depends on the amount of data stored on the iPad and the speed of your internet connection. Just let the process complete and don't pause or lose your Wi-Fi connection.

Move an old iPad to a new iPad using iTunes

You can also transfer data from an old iPad to a new iPad with the help of iTunes. This is the old way as iPads need to be connected to a computer. However, it works just fine if you don't have iCloud or a fast internet connection.

With the old iPad

1. Introduce iTunes and connect the old iPad to the computer.

2. Right-click on the iPad in the iTunes sidebar and choose Backup.

3. Let iTunes finish the iPad backup, keep iTunes open, but disconnect the old iPad from the computer

With the new iPad

1. Turn on the new iPad and the Set Up iPad screen, choose to Restore from iTunes Backup, and then tap next.

2. Connect the iPad to the computer and within iTunes choose the latest backup from the restore menu

3. Click next and allow iTunes to restore. Do not disconnect the iPad till the allocation is complete and the iPad has started over.

Restoring from iTunes may be faster than restoring from iCloud, depending on the size of your backups and the speed of your internet connection. Even so, migrating with iCloud is the easiest and therefore the most recommended.

Note: If you've already set up your new iPad, you can easily return to the original settings and the settings screen required for the transfer by tapping Settings> General> Reset> Erase All Contents and Settings. This will reset every iOS device to factory default. This will delete the whole thing on the iPad.

SIRI

How to activate and use Siri on your iPad to ask questions, give commands, and more

Before Alexa even existed, Siri was the ubiquitous digital assistant of the iPhone. But you don't have to limit your Siri conversations to your phone; it works on the iPad too.

And thanks to the intelligent integration, only one reacts when you activate Siri near both iOS devices, so you won't hear the answer in stereo.

Before using Siri on your iPad, however, you'll need to make sure it's enabled and configured exactly the way you want it to be. Do it this way.

How to permit Siri on your iPad

Launch the Settings app, and then tap Siri & Search. Most of the settings on this page apply to Siri.

You can also modify Siri's voice and language on this page.

Another important setting controls what happens when you press the Home or Power button. When you press Home or Power for Siri, do you want Siri to hear your voice for a question, or do you just have your question typed? To choose between these options, do the following:

1. Start the Settings app and then tap on "Accessibility".

2. Touch Siri.

3. If you want the Home or Power button to start Siri in write-only mode, enable Write to Siri by sliding the button to the right. If you want to talk to Siri using the Home or Power button, keep it turned off.

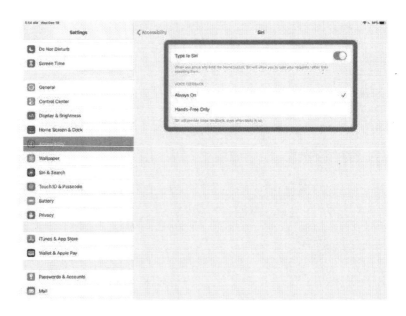

How to use Siri on iPad

Once you've enabled and configured Siri, you can start the wizard by saying "Hey Siri," or pressing and holding the Home or Power button until the Siri screen appears.

In either case, you can now give an order or ask a question.

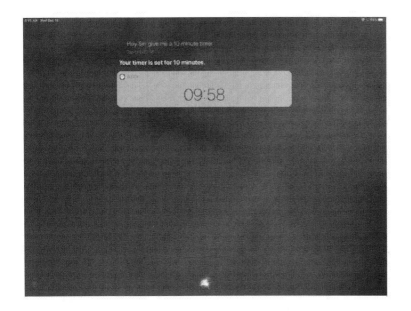

117

APPLE PAY

Set up and use Apple Pay for in-app purchases and fast online payments

While Apple Pay may be more useful for iPhone users on the go, the feature is fully functional on iPads as well.

There are many ways to use Apple Pay on your iPad – this is how it's done.

Apple Pay works on your iPad

The principal way you can use Apple Pay on your iPad is to set it up with Touch ID, which permits you to use it for in-app purchases and online at contributing stores.

Even though you probably won't be using your iPad for in-store shopping, Apple Pay is still useful for its other benefits: accessing your transaction history, purchasing transit tickets, and browsing the App Store.

Also note that when you sync Apple Pay through your iCloud account, the same cards you add to your iPad will also appear on your other devices.

Set up Apple Pay on your iPad

1. Go to Settings.

2. on the fourth set of options, scroll down to Wallet & Apple Pay.

3. Touch the blue "Add Card" option.

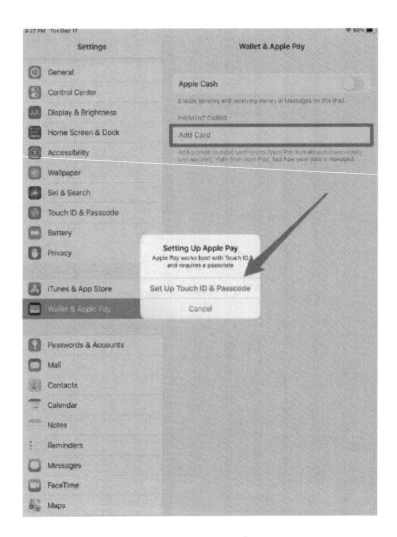

4. If you haven't set up Touch ID yet, you may be prompted to do so at this point. Your settings will forward you to the Touch ID & Passcode section, in which you have to activate the "Apple Pay" switch. Touch or slide your finger to change from gray to green.

5. Setup walks you through the steps to set up your Touch ID for use with Apple Pay. Follow the instructions by placing your finger on the home button and setting a password.

6. When you're done, return to the Wallet and Apple Pay section, where you can now add a card under Payment Cards.

7. A pop-up window will open. Touch "Next".

8. Choose your card type and place your card in the frame or enter your information manually. Read and accept the terms and conditions and complete the installation instructions.

9. When done, you should receive a notification that your newly added card is ready for Apple Pay. When you touch a card, you'll see your banking information as well as a list of your most recent Apple Pay transactions.

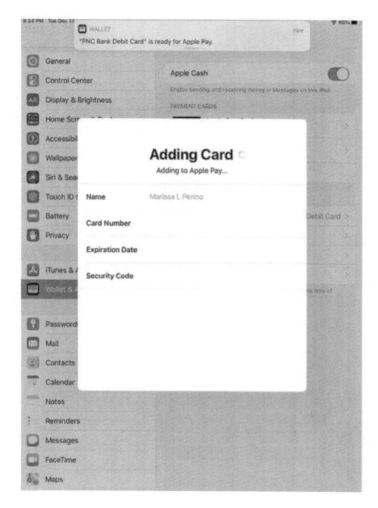

You can also configure your standard transactions on this page. This includes choosing your standard card and updating your delivery address and contact information for in-app and online purchases.

Use Apple Pay on your iPad

1. Just like on your iPhone or Mac, Apple Pay can be used for both in-app purchases and online orders. For the latter, look for the Apple logo followed by "Pay," which usually appears in black near the payment options.

2. Tapping the Apple Pay option will bring up a pop-up window for you to choose your card. Your delivery address and contact information are entered automatically so that you can also skip all steps of an online expense. Use Touch ID to finish the purchase.

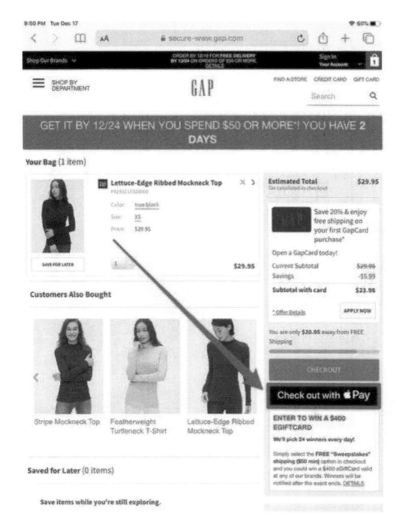

3. As with your iPhone, you can access Apple Pay to make in-app purchases. When you're ready to pay in a participating app, you should find the Apple Pay option too. This option is used in many popular applications including grocery ordering services, transit systems, and more.

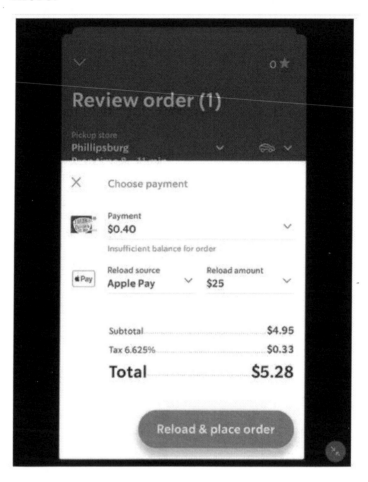

HOW TO SET UP ICLOUD ON IPAD

iCloud is one of the most important functions that connect your various iOS devices. Not only can you use it to back up and restore your iPad without connecting it to your PC, but you can also access the same notes, calendar, reminders, and contacts on your iPhone, iPad, or your laptop's web browser. You can also share documents in iWork Suite and share photos through Photo Stream. Typically, you'd set up iCloud when you set up your iPad. However, if you skipped this step, you can always set up iCloud.

1. Go to iPad Settings (it's the icon that looks like the gears are spinning).
2. Scroll down the menu on the left, find iCloud, and tap on it.

3. If iCloud is already set up, your Apple ID will appear next to the account. Otherwise, tap Account and set up iCloud by entering your Apple ID and password. You can also choose an email address for your iCloud email account.

Here are some of the features of iCloud. The activated functions are displayed with a green switch. You can activate the functions simply by touching the switch.

iCloud functions

- **Mail**. Choosing an email address for your iCloud account will enable an iCloud email for your iPad. With this option enabled, you can read the email from iCloud through the Mail app. You can check that an email address has been set up by tapping Account.

Note: Although your Apple ID might be your email address, the iCloud email is different from your Apple ID. Your iCloud email address ends with "@ icloud.com".

- **Contacts**. Your contact list is saved on iCloud.com. If you've enabled Contacts for another iOS device (iPhone, etc.), your contact list will be synced between devices.

- **Calendar**. With the calendar, you can mark events and meetings and keep them synchronized on all your devices. You can even schedule meetings with Siri.

- **Safari.** When you turn on Safari in iCloud, you can open a webpage on your iPad and then switch to another device like your laptop or iPhone and easily open the same page.

- **Notes**. The Notes app is an inordinate way to share facts between devices. You can set up multiple notes. When enabled, you can access Notes on iCloud.com and other devices.

- **Keychain**. One of the newest features of iCloud is the ability to store your passwords and credit cards in the cloud so you can easily log into your accounts regardless of your device. If you want to enable this feature, you may need to verify access to your other devices. So make sure your iPhone and any other keychain connected devices are ready.

- **Photos**. Picture Stream is an inordinate way to share pictures with friends and family. It also syncs your latest photos between your iOS devices.

- **Documents and data**. An important function of iCloud is the ability to exchange information between devices. In this setting, you can choose whether the iPad uses iCloud to store documents on the Internet. If you want to keep your documents secretive, you can turn this setting off. You can also choose specific applications to share data with iCloud, although the application must support iCloud sharing.

- **Find my iPad.** With Find My iPad, one of the most important functions of iCloud, you can locate your iPad via GPS or location services; play a sound on the iPad. This is useful when trying to locate it in your home. Turn on Lost Mode, which will lock your iPad, and erase all data on your iPad.

- **Storage and backup.** Another important feature of iCloud is the ability to back up data on your iPad. Entering this setting will allow you to set up an automatic backup that occurs when you plug in your iPad for charging. You can also back up your iPad manually. This is a good idea if you've just turned on backups. Whenever you need to buy a new iPad or do a factory reset on your current iPad, when you set up the iPad you will be asked whether or not you want to reinstate from a backup.

IPADOS 14 TIPS AND TRICKS

With the summary of the iPadOS 13 last year, Apple stepped up its energies to market the iPad as an output device. It greatly improved multitasking performance, introduced desktop-class internet surfing, added support for external drives, and more. The Cupertino-based tech giant even went so deep as to implement complete trackpad and mouse support. This year, iPadOS 14 brings more additions and improvements to the native iPad apps and the operating system in general. If you've just upgraded your iPad to iPadOS 14, this book is going to go over the best tips and tricks you can do right away.

Stack widgets in the Today view

IPadOS 14 includes detailed, customizable, and redesigned widgets in the Today view.

There is also a smart stack of widgets that rotate automatically based on usage patterns. You can manage the widgets by dragging the Today view.

However, you can also reduce the clutter in Today's view by stacking widgets instead of removing them. Simply drag widgets of similar size over each other. They then work similarly to the standard smart stack in terms of functionality.

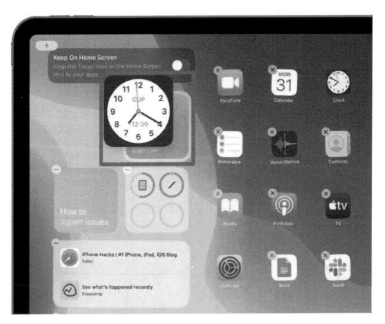

Move apps from anywhere

IPadOS 14 made it a lot easier to move your home screen apps around. Instead of holding down an app's icon, simply press and hold an empty area on the home screen for a fraction of a second. This also applies to the Today view.

Open universal search websites

The iPadOS 14 search function has been visually redesigned so that it is similar to Spotlight search on the Mac. It also works faster, offers better suggestions, and helps you load relevant results quickly.

This new "universal" search doubles as an address bar. Just enter in a website's URL and tap Go to seamlessly load it into a new Safari tab.

Writing instead of typing

The iPadOS 14 comes with a new addition called Scribble. If you have an Apple Pencil, just write anywhere with a text box, Scribble will automatically convert your handwriting to typed text.

For instance, you can now type your inquiries into Universal Search or Safari deprived of having to search through the on-screen keyboard. The possibilities that Scribble offers are endless.

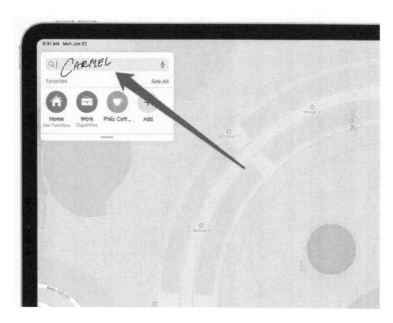

You can also use Scribble in the Notes application. Just select the scribble pen from the toolbox (the one with the letter "A") and you're done.

Drag apps to multitask

No, have you found a solution for the iPad? It is not a worry. With a keyboard attached to your iPad, just press Command + Spacebar to open Universal Search. Then find the application and drag it out of the results window to open it in Split-View or Slide Over.

This was possible in iPadOS 13 as well, but it's an incredibly useful (and lesser-known) feature worth mentioning again.

Draw precise shapes

Drawing precise shapes with an apple pencil in the Notes app is a breeze. Just start drawing and hold down Apple Pencil at the end. IPadOS 14 recognizes that the shape is automatically adjusted. This works for many shapes like lines, circles, rectangles, pentagons, etc.

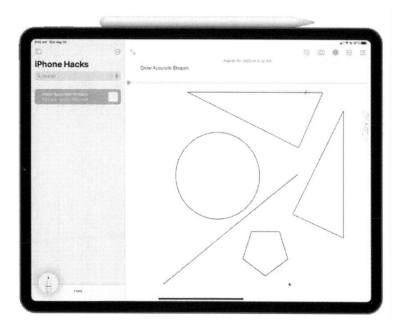

Identify invasive privacy applications

IPadOS 14 introduced numerous privacy and security-oriented features that make it much more difficult for apps to sniff around on your iPad. One of these features will notify you when an app is using the camera or microphone as a green or orange dot in the iPad's status bar.

Simply open the Control Center to determine the exact application that your camera or microphone is using (or has recently used).

Choose the handwritten text.

On iPadOS 14, you will find a list of the important information that you have rights to assignments. Just double-tap and use the selection controls to highlight the text as needed.

To make things even better, you can copy and paste the handwriting into other applications

Use Scribble gestures

With iPadOS 14, Scribble is very convenient to use with several unique and fun Apple Pencil gestures. These are the best:

- **Scratches:** Eliminate Words.
- **Circle:** Select a word, phrase, or paragraph.
- **Cut:** create or remove spaces.

Translate languages in Safari

Surprisingly, iPadOS 14 didn't get the new iOS 14 translator app. However, you can translate someone else's website in Safari: open Safari's aA menu, then select Translate to English.

Access Universal search without a keyboard

The redesigned "Universal" search is so good at finding apps, files, and photos that it's worth using anywhere. But without a keyboard, you're just limited to the home screen, right? Fortunately, there is a workaround: AssistiveTouch.

Go to Settings> Accessibility> Touch> AssistiveTouch. Then activate Assistive Touch and link Spotlight as a single-touch, double-touch, or activation push gesture.

You can then point to the AssistiveTouch floating circle to have Universal Search appear whenever and wherever you want.

Drag and drop items into the sidebar

You must have noticed the new sidebars in the iPadOS 14 native apps like Photos, Shortcuts, and Voice Notes. No solo makes navigation easier. Instead, you can use them to move things around easily. For example, you can drag and drop pictures into albums in the Photos sidebar.

With the Files app, you can also use the sidebar to move files. However, you can do this on iPadOS 13 as well.

Pin iMessage conversations

Are you using iMessage on the iPad? Reaching your favorite conversations just got easier. Swipe right a conversation thread and tap the pin icon. You can have a total of nine pinned conversations at the same time.

Use Apple Music AutoPlay

IPadOS 14 has a redesigned music app with better navigation and an impressive full-screen player. It also has a new autoplay function that allows music to be played even after an album or playlist has ended. Open the "Next" list to enable or disable the feature.

Take mirrored selfies

Would you rather take selfies on the iPad? Prevent them from spinning the other way by going to Settings> Camera and then checking the Front Mirror Camera option.

Use of rapid rotation of images in files

You can now rotate pictures in the Files app without opening them. Touch and hold an image and choose Rotate Left or Rotate Right as needed.

Uncheck worksheet sharing suggestions

IPadOS 13 has started adding contact suggestions at the top of sheet sharing. If you don't like the extra clutter, iPadOS 14 can help you remove it easily. To do this, go to Settings> Siri & Search and toggle the switch next to Suggestions while sharing.

Enhance your voice memos

The new Voice Memo application is a quick way to improve the quality of your recorded voice memos by removing background noise and echoes. Go to the Edit Recording screen and then quickly tap the Enhance Magic Wand Recording icon.

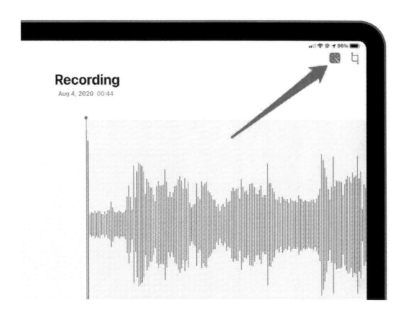

Open the Emoji Selector

If you are using a smart keyboard or a magic keyboard, just tap the globe button to bring up a sleek emoji image where the cursor is located. This works in any text area.

Send audio messages with Siri

Fortunately, Siri no longer takes over the giant iPad screen every time you call it up. To round off the new compact design, it's a lot smarter too. For example, you can ask it to record an audio message and send it to contact by saying Send an audio message to [contact name]. Once you finish recording, say Send.

Put important photos in albums

The Photos app in iPadOS 14 now offers the best conceivable photo experience with astonishing zoom in/out cartoons and quicker navigation thanks to the new sidebar.

But did you know that you can also set any photo as a key photo in an album? Long press your favorite photograph and tap Make Key Photo.

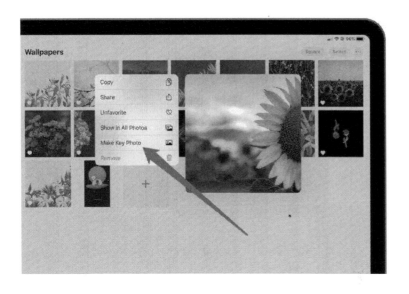

Limit access to the photo library

With iPadOS 14, you don't have to give third-party apps full access to your entire photo library. Instead, you can limit the exposure of individual photos or albums as needed. Go to Settings> Privacy> Photos to manage photo permissions.

Discard call notifications without rejecting them

The FaceTime or iPhone notifications for incoming calls from IPadOS 14 won't hijack your entire screen ... Finally! But did you know that you can reject calls without rejecting them? Just slide it up and callers won't notice!

Search for apps in the iPad storage

The iPad storage management screen now has a built-in search icon. Touch it to filter apps by title.

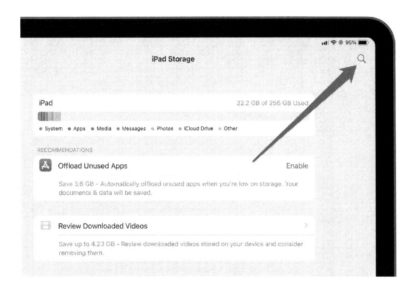

Adjust the opacity of the screenshot

Do you take a lot of screenshots on the iPad? Here's a great tip: you can use the new Opacity slider in the top right of the screen to adjust the opacity. It is particularly useful for improving the visibility of annotations in noisy screenshots.

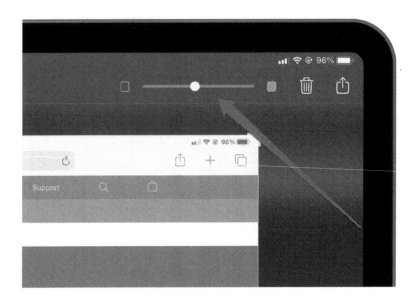

Add captions

Another cool tip from the Photos app: swipe up while viewing a photo and add your captions. They'll also sync with other devices if you've turned on iCloud Photos.

Change the video quality in the camera application

Go to Settings> Camera> Record Video, toggle the switch next to Video Format Control, and you don't need to go to the Settings app to change the resolution while recording the video. Instead, tap the Resolution/fps indicator in the Camera app to scroll through the available quality settings.

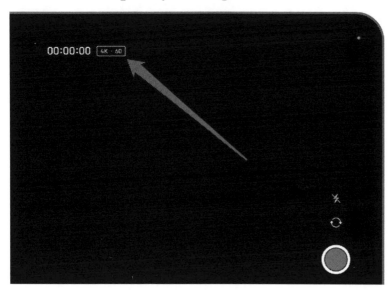

Double-tap to drag

If you use a magic keyboard with a trackpad, instead of tapping and dragging, you can drag items (like icons on the home screen) with a simple double-click.

Go to Settings> Accessibility> Pointer Controls> Double-tap to drag. Then select Without Draw Lock or With Draw Lock.

Watch YouTube in 4K

IPadOS 14 supports the Google VP9 codec. That means you can finally watch YouTube videos in 4K on your iPad!

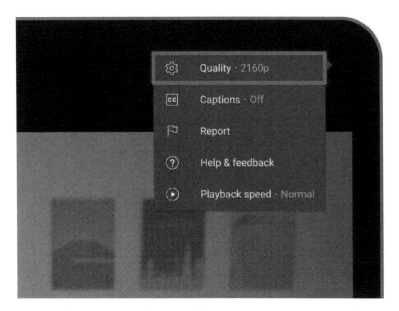

Open the Quality menu while watching a video in the YouTube app. The 2160p option should be listed.

Set the default email client and browser

Safari has been significantly improved in iPadOS 14 with better data protection regulations, a built-in translation module, and a faster JavaScript engine. However, this hasn't stopped Apple from changing the default browsers.

For example, if you like Google Chrome, you can make it the default browser on the iPad. Go to Settings> Chrome> Default Browser App and choose Chrome from the next menu.

This also applies to email clients, where you can switch to Gmail or Microsoft Outlook if you prefer those to the native email app.

View history stacks

If you're buried in multiple pages of a native app, just hold down the Back option to bring up a stack of previous pages. Select one for quick access.

Enable or disable exact location

With iPadOS 14, you can choose whether or not an application should have access to your exact location. Just go to Settings> Privacy> Location Services. Select an app and use the slider next to a precise location to enable or disable it.

Switch to Dumb Stack

Are you annoyed by the auto-rotate feature in the Smart Widget Stack? Press and hold the stack, select Edit Stack, then toggle the switch next to Smart Rotate to prevent this from happening.

Hide Mac address

IPadOS 14 allows you to improve your privacy by masking your iPad's MAC address. In the Settings app, go to the Wi-Fi screen, tap a Wi-Fi network, and toggle the switch next to Home Address.

Submit ETA with Siri

You can also share your ETA with other people using Siri. While using the mapping application, say Hey Siri, share my ETA with [contact name] to get your E.T.A. with a contact.

Printed in Great Britain
by Amazon